JOURNEY INTO MARRIAGE

Journey Into Marriage

YVONNE WARREN

KINGSWAY PUBLICATIONS
EASTBOURNE

Unless otherwise indicated, biblical
quotations are from the New International Version
© 1973, 1978, 1984 by the
International Bible Society

Quotations from the Alternative Service Book are
copyright © The Central Board of Finance of the
Church of England 1980 and are used by permission.

Front cover photo: Tony Stone Photolibrary – London

ISBN 0 86065 984 4

Printed in Great Britain for
KINGSWAY PUBLICATIONS LTD
Lottbridge Drove, Eastbourne, E Sussex BN23 6NT by
Clays Ltd, St Ives plc
Typeset by J&L Composition Ltd, Filey, North Yorkshire

Contents

He's everything I've ever dreamed of . . .

Good-looking and very sexy.
Kind and thoughtful.
Fun to be with.
Easy to talk to.
Makes me feel good.
And he's a Christian as well!

I can't believe it's true . . .

She laughs at all my jokes.
She's fabulous to look at.
I can tell her anything.
She gets on with my mum.
She's good with my mates.
And she goes to church as well!

. . . We love each other and we're planning to get married shortly.

This book is written to help Christian couples think through their relationship and to help them prepare for a life-long commitment together in marriage, with all its joys and pains. Your relationship is unique—unlike anyone else's. Because of that there will be no stories of other marriages to model on. Instead you will have the chance to explore *your* relationship and see what you and God want it to be like.

May God bless you as you read through this together.

I

Expectations

As you look beyond the wedding day to your life together, you will have high hopes—

✠ that you will be happy

✠ that sex will be good and satisfying

✠ that you will have enough money to do the things you want

✠ if you have children, that they will grow up and cause few problems

✠ that your partner will always be there for you

✠ that your love for each other will never change

✠ that because Jesus is in your life there won't be any conflicts that you can't manage

It is good to have high expectations and it is hard to imagine how things could change because you both feel so much in love.

Yet you do need to look at the reality of marriage today, and to think through what it means for the two of you to get married.

2

Reality

More than one in three marriages ends in divorce—and sadly there are many Christian marriages to be counted among them. Attitudes to marriage have changed and the Christian couple can get caught up in these attitudes without realising it. Here are some modern views and attitudes which may affect us:

✠ *There is no need for permanence.* When something is old you throw it away. This can affect relationships too.

✠ *Divorce is easy.* This discourages people from staying with a problem and aiming to work through it.

✠ *We have high expectations of happiness.* This makes us unprepared for difficulties and problems.

✠ *Sex should be completely fulfilling.* This makes it hard to adjust if it isn't.

✢ *We desire higher standards of living.* This leads to wanting more in terms of money and possessions and makes men and women put more effort into developing their careers than in developing their relationship.

✢ *We want children who won't cause too much disruption in the family.* Mothers can feel that looking after children is not enough of a worthwhile job.

✢ *We want equality of men and women.* This can make it difficult for men and women to know what their roles should be in marriage.

✢ *We accept a very pressurised work situation.* This gives little time for the couple and for family life.

✢ *Life is about 'me first'.* This makes it hard to put your partner first.

✢ *God is not concerned with marriage.* This can lead to keeping 'ordinary life' and our relationship with God completely separate.

These are the world's attitudes. But couples also come into marriage with their own personal needs and fears—conscious and unconscious—which will have been formed during childhood experiences.

There is the need to be—

> accepted
> loved
> valued
> made to feel secure

These needs can put an enormous strain on any relationship. This book will lead you through the different areas of your life together. As you discuss them, look at the ones that you feel may be more difficult for you to handle. Talk over each one from every angle, then bring that part of your relationship to God for his love and grace to surround you in it.

But first of all, let us look at where God is in all of this. Marriage and sex are his ideas, right from when he made Eve to be a companion for Adam. Together Adam and Eve made a complete fit—both emotionally, physically, and as a working team. God has always been interested in marriage, that relationship of one man with one woman to the end of their life together. In the Gospels Jesus spells out God's concern when, at the wedding in Cana in Galilee, he reiterated God's words:

> For this reason a man will leave his father and mother and unite with his wife, and the two will become one . . . Man must not separate, then, what God has joined together (Matthew 19:5–6).

3
God's Plan for Your Marriage

God's idea of marriage is that it should be:

Permanent

His plan is for a life-long committed relationship which will stretch into the distance for ten, twenty, thirty, forty years—however long you live. Right through the Bible we see God's desire for this, as well as the problems created when marriage is not treated seriously.

Companionable

God knew that even though Adam had an open relationship with him, he needed a fellow human being to relate to him and to be a heart companion. At the centre of marriage is this deep love and companionship between a man and a woman who are different and yet complementary, so that they can be to each other in so many ways the 'other half'.

Deeply pleasurable

God has given the gift of sex in marriage first and foremost so that you can express your deep love for each other in the physical act of sexual intercourse. There you can delight in each other's bodies in an intimate way that is just for the two of you, keeping to God's plan to restrict sexual intercourse to marriage.

Procreative

God's plan is that this planet should be populated, and that children should be brought up in loving and secure families.

Supportive

'For richer, for poorer; in sickness and in health; till death us do part.' Whatever the circumstances, there is to be a readiness to support and care for each other and to work through the good and bad times so that you mature as individuals and as a couple.

This is God's plan for your marriage.

Now let us look in more detail at the different areas of marriage and see how God's plan can work out in practical ways. At the end of each section there will be suggested discussion points for you to use together

4

Love

B eing in love is a wonderful and glorious experience, where the grass seems greener and the sky more blue, and everything in the garden is lovely.

That state of bliss cannot last. It may last until after the honeymoon (though the honeymoon time itself can sometimes be less than blissful) or it may go on longer, but either way the fact of living every day of your life with someone will eventually bring you down to earth!

It may be because one of you squeezes the toothpaste tube in the middle and the other from the bottom, or one of you leaves clothes lying on the floor and the other is oppressively tidy. Living in the same house will soon show up the other side of the fantastic person you are married to, and little irritations and annoyances will creep in. Before long, the person sharing your bed may seem like a stranger.

This early stage is probably the most important time in your married life, because you will begin to see each other without the rose-tinted glasses of a new and romantic relationship. You will see each other's good and bad points, strengths and weaknesses; you will see that you are both human and therefore fallible and vulnerable. This is when the state of 'loving' can take over from that of 'being in love'.

We speak of God as 'the God of love', so let us see what the Bible says love is:

Love is patient and kind; it is not jealous or conceited or proud; love is not ill-mannered or selfish or irritable; love does not keep a record of wrongs; love is not happy with evil, but is happy with the truth. Love never gives up, and its faith, hope, and patience never fail. Love is eternal (1 Corinthians 13:4–8).

In this passage we see that love is about—

✛ accepting the other person by being patient and kind

✛ valuing the other person by not being conceited, rude, or ill-mannered

✛ making the other person feel secure by not keeping a record of wrongs.

Love never gives up. In a Christian marriage, where a couple believe God has brought them together, they will seek every way possible to work through problems. This will mean asking for God's help, and sometimes that of other people too.

Love is not jealous. It may be that because of a difficult childhood or a previous disappointment in love one of you feels insecure and finds it hard to love and to believe that you are loved. Possessiveness may creep in and disrupt your life, so that you become very jealous of your partner's friends or work colleagues. Sometimes a person needs help to work through this. In a relationship of love, the insecure partner can learn to feel secure and loved and can work through the painful experiences of the past. But this needs time and commitment from both.

This sort of love is hard to sustain, for this is what perfect love is, and none of us is perfect except Jesus. This picture of love describes Jesus and his sort of love completely.

Jesus showed his love by leaving the glories of heaven to share the poverty and degradation of ordinary men and women, so that he could point them to God. The life of Jesus was one of total sacrifice in his works of healing, teaching and, supremely, his death on the cross. There Jesus built the bridge for us to find salvation and forgiveness, and through the gift of his Holy Spirit to experience eternal life.

This pattern of loving is one that we are asked to follow—and though we cannot be perfect as Jesus was, at the heart of any marriage should be the desire to put the other person first, to be prepared to give and not always to take. That is the pattern of sacrificial love that God desires in your relationship.

It is as you come to Jesus, loving each other, making a mess of it sometimes but wanting the sort of love described in 1 Corinthians 13 to be in your marriage, that Jesus promises to come alongside and to put his love into you, to teach you to love not only him but each other in this way. You may need more help from your pastor or vicar to understand what the love of Jesus is.

'Love never gives up, and its faith, hope, and patience never fail. Love is eternal.' Yes, the rose-tinted glasses may be off, but in the reality of seeing each other more as you really are you can begin to learn to love each other with a Christ-like love. This may be painful at times, but will bring growth and maturity to your relationship, enabling it to stand up to all that is thrown at it from outside. You do have the whole of your lives to work at this.

Discussion points

1. In the light of 1 Corinthians 13:4–8 how does your love for each other measure up? Are you seeing beyond the rose-tinted spectacles?
2. Take each section of the passage in turn and talk about how patient you are, how kind, how easily able to forget wrongs, and so on.
3. What is going to be the hardest part of loving for you?
4. What is going to be the easiest part? Discuss your differences.
5. Are you prepared to put your partner's wishes before your own in order to please, even when doing so conflicts with your own wishes?
6. How well can you cope with your partner's friends and work colleagues?
7. How well do you cope with each other's families?
8. How well do you cope with each other's choice of leisure pursuits?
9. How secure do you feel in your partner's love for you?

5
Commitment

———❦❦❦❦❦———

We have seen that God's plan for your marriage is that it should be a permanent one. For this to happen there needs to be a deep sense of commitment, not only to each other but to the relationship itself. What does that mean?

It means that, after your commitment to God, your marriage relationship should come first. In terms of importance your commitments in life would look a bit like this:

GOD
YOUR MARRIAGE
CHILDREN
WORK
CHURCH, FAMILY AND FRIENDS
OTHER INTERESTS

In Matthew 19:5 we read: 'And God said, "For this reason a man will leave his father and mother and unite with his wife."' Marriage is about forming a new relationship, a new family. In doing this you will be bringing your models of family life from your past and your thoughts and feelings about how families should be. As you share together in this you will be forming your own new family, which will be unique.

It is sometimes hard for you not to feel dependent, still, on Mum and Dad. It may be too that for a short while you will have to live with one set of parents, but even if that is the case it is important that emotionally you 'leave' your parents so that you can sort out your own relationship. For you are no longer your parents' little girl or little boy. You have adult responsibilities and commitments.

It may well be that Mum cooks better than your wife, or Dad does the decorating better than your husband, but it's *your* life, *your* relationship that matters most now. Better to work and strive together in partnership, sometimes not getting it right, than to feel the anger and frustration of intrusive in-laws who can't let their children go.

Instead here is a marvellous chance of embarking on a different relationship with your parents— one that is on the adult level of sharing and mutuality.

Commitment is also about the special, unique relationship of the one-man and one-woman bond. In our society of low moral standards, there are all sorts of temptations for the unwary. In the wedding service you promise to each other to keep yourself 'only unto him/her'. This is a promise of sexual and emotional constancy and fidelity. Christians—the same as others—sometimes find their eyes or minds straying to a pretty face or handsome body. All Christians need to pray that the Lord will help them to keep faithful to their marriage vows.

But how can you deal with people or situations that intrude? In the first year of marriage it is essential to be quite 'selfish' as a couple. That is not to say that you cut yourselves off from everyone and everything and live on a desert island for a year—as nice as that thought may be. No, it means that for the first year you spend time and energy on working at your relationship, on learning to be responsible for the home maintenance, and in getting to know each other intimately. Work, church and other activities should be kept to an acceptable minimum as you learn to cope with each other's temperaments, personalities and needs.

It is during this year that you will discover whether you feel in-laws are too intrusive, or if you feel that your needs are being put second to the needs of others. You will be aware of how work pressures affect your married life. You will learn how to cope with each other's friends and leisure pursuits. In this year you will need to work out compromises so that the essential commitment that is needed for both to feel secure in the marriage will be intact.

A more difficult situation is deciding how to handle those straying eyes and thoughts when either one of you feels attracted to someone else. We live in a sex-mad society which thrusts other people's sexual attributes into our consciousness all the time. There are no quick answers. But there are some safeguards which will help to keep you faithful to each other 'as long as you both shall live'.

1. Work hard at your marriage. Give it top priority.
2. Spend time talking, sharing, and loving each other.
3. See your relationship as a life-long commitment, remembering that you will always have more to learn about each other.
4. Keep away from heavy emotional involvement with people of the opposite sex, unless you are both involved equally together.
5. Make sure that nothing and no one is allowed to come between the two of you.

6. Pray that God will protect your relationship and help you to work at being a unit.
7. If you are tempted, walk away fast, pray, and seek help. Look at your relationship to see where it is lacking, and then both look at how you can work on it together.

Discussion points

1. How do you think your parents see themselves in your total relationship? In what ways do you see that changing?
2. What are your plans for your first year together? What could you give up (if you need to) in order to have more time just for the two of you?
3. You both may have single friends who will feel left out by you now that you are married. Or you may feel there are friends who are too intrusive in your new life together. How will you manage this?
4. Are you completely committed to making this relationship work, or do you still have reservations?
5. How will you deal with the situation when one or other of you feels a strong attraction to someone else? How can you avoid being too possessive, and yet remain faithful?

6
Roles

E quality of opportunity is the cry. Equal rights for women! Equal pay for women! And how right that is. Now, as never before, a couple has the chance to decide what roles, duties and decisions should be taken by whom. There is no need for stereotyping, but a chance for you to do things your way. Each of you will, however, bring to your marriage your own ideas about what husbands do and what wives do, which you will have learned from your own and other families you know. Before your marriage you may talk about sharing and equality, but after marriage you may feel very peeved if your husband doesn't organise the finances as your father always did, or if your wife doesn't do all the shopping because her mother never did.

There is no manual which lays down the husband's role or the wife's role. How do you know what each should do? Who does the cooking when both have been out at work all day? Who puts the dustbins out, does the shopping, looks after the garden, cleans the house? Who writes letters, sends birthday cards, gets the car filled up with petrol? You have no guidelines except your own family backgrounds, your friends' suggestions, and your own view of yourselves.

It is helpful to have a list of the different jobs that have to be done and to decide who will do what. After marriage you can change it if work routine means that one of you can't do a particular chore while the other can. In marriage you need to be flexible and prepared to change roles around to ensure that you always feel comfortable with what you are expected to do. Over the years things may change again as circumstances alter.

There will need to be plenty of discussion. It is always hard to change what has been a known way of doing things, but with patience, love and compromise it is possible. Again, you have plenty of time—a lifetime in fact!

A biblical view of roles is seen in Ephesians 5:21–33, which offers a Christian couple some guidelines.

Submit yourselves to one another because of your reverence for Christ. Wives, submit to your husbands as to the Lord. For a husband has authority over his wife just as Christ has authority over the church; and Christ is himself the Saviour of the church, his body. And so wives must submit completely to their husbands just as the church submits itself to Christ.

Husbands, love your wives just as Christ loved the church and gave his life for it. . . . Men ought to love their wives just as they love their own bodies. A man who loves his wife loves himself. . . . As the scripture says, 'For this reason a man will leave his father and mother and unite with his wife, and the two will become one' . . . every husband must love his wife as himself, and every wife must respect her husband.

A wife may not like the idea of her husband having authority over her and her having to submit to him. But notice first that both are asked to submit to each other because of their reverence for Jesus Christ. This surely means having a respect and concern for each other—respecting each as a unique person, made in the image of God, who has been given gifts and talents to be used not only in the service of God, but also within your relationship. Respecting is about knowing and valuing each other for what you can and do bring to the marriage. It also means accepting the things that you can't do—accepting the inadequacies and the weaknesses.

Jesus went to the cross for the sins of the world and, through that act and his resurrection, he brought into being the church. That same sort of love, expressed through sacrifice and self-giving, is to be the sort of love a husband has for his wife. And as the church loves and submits to Jesus because of all he has done, so the wife is asked to submit to her husband—not in a way which demeans her as a person, but out of love for him and all that he is called to be for her.

This love and respect for one another will enable you to be more truly a man and more truly a woman. Glory in your differences, both physical and emotional, and release each other in love to be yourselves. God loves you both equally.

Discussion points

1. What role patterns were in place in the homes you grew up in? Discuss together the assumptions you have grown up with. Will yours be different?

2. Are you prepared to take on responsibilities in your marriage that in the past you have associated with the other sex?
3. Do you have a problem with the idea of a wife 'submitting' to her husband?
4. Does the idea of a husband loving his wife 'as Christ loved the church' seem realistic?

7
Money

━━━━━━━━∞∞∞∞∞∞━━━━━━━━

M oney is not the root of all evil, as is so often quoted. What 1 Timothy 6:10 actually says is that 'the love of money is the root of all evil'. We all know that money is necessary, yet it can be a cause of conflict and marriage breakdown. You live in a materialistic society where money speaks of:

✣ your status in society

✣ how valued you feel

✣ how well you are doing

✣ the freedom to live as you want

✣ being able to buy new possessions

✣ keeping up with your peer group

And in this money-oriented society problems can arise in a marriage when:

✤ a husband is not happy if his wife earns more than he does

✤ one partner is careful with money and the other liberal

✤ one partner is made redundant, is unable to find work or is unable to work through illness

✤ a wife stops earning to have a child

✤ it is impossible to make ends meet

✤ debts increase

✤ God is left out of the financial area of life

Perhaps you have already discussed how you will organise your finances. You may even have worked out a budget so that you have a clear idea before you are married of what your probable income and expenditure will be. Using a budget account to work out likely weekly, monthly and annual expenditure will take a lot of pressure off you both. It is essential that you are both aware of how much you each earn and what your

	Rent or mort-gage	House-keeping	Major house-hold bills	Loans	Car	Spend-ing money	Work	Gifts to charity	Holi-days & Xmas	Savings
Money carried over from last last sheet										
Wages/salary to add in										
New total in hand										

Daily spending details											
	S										
	S										
	M										
	T										
	W										
	T										
	F										
Total to carry over to next sheet											

SAMPLE BUDGET SHEET

expenditure is, so that you know how much you will have left over for presents, holidays, leisure pursuits and savings. You could use a sheet like the example given as one way of doing this.

Making a will in case one of you dies will take off any pressure for the remaining partner, who would have so much to deal with in the middle of such a tragedy.

Many people find themselves getting into serious debt these days. Hire purchase agreements, high interest rates on mortgages and the availability of credit cards, can all combine to produce a vicious circle of borrowing, and then borrowing more to pay off the debts.

Sit down together and look at who will be in charge of your finances. Decide whether to have separate bank accounts, so that you can have your own individual money for presents, or a joint account, or maybe both.

Make a budget for three months, or even better for the first year. This will help you have a clear idea of your expenses.

What insurances will you take out on property or your lives?

Making these decisions together will help you feel responsible and in control, and will engender a sense of security in your relationship. This will be particularly important when only one of you is earning.

See money as a tool to help you live, but not as the main need in your marriage. And don't be afraid to ask advice from the experts. Local banks are often willing to advise their customers, or you may feel you need the help of a professional accountant.

And keep away from money-lenders. Many a young couple have been shipwrecked by the loan sharks, not reading the small print and so getting deeper and deeper into debt.

Whether you have to count every penny, or have inherited a fortune, the responsibility for your joint finances is now yours. You may know the joy of being able to help others, or the delight of finding a much-needed bargain. You may need to save hard for a treat, or decide that you can't afford it this time.

Money is God's business. 'All the silver and gold of the world is mine' (Haggai 2:8). God wants to be involved in the financial area of your life as in every other area. Some Christians like to give God a tenth of all they earn right from the beginning, as a way of saying that the money is his and his gift to them. It shows they trust him fully to provide for all their needs. This began in the Old Testament as a way for the people of God to acknowledge that everything they have is given them by God and is to be used for his glory.

Discussion points

1. How important is money to you? Have you always had enough, or have you been used to 'making do'?
2. How has your faith in God affected your financial affairs? Discuss the different ways in which you have both responded to his call on your money.
3. Discuss the question of tithing. Is this something you plan to do together?
4. Are you good at saving? What are your plans for saving in the future?

8
Work

Work has always been important. When God made Adam and Eve he made them not just to be together and enjoy each other's company, but also to work and look after the land he had put them in. So through the ages it has always been that both men and women have needed to use their gifts and creative energy in order to find fulfilment and a sense of purpose and satisfaction. We may work for many reasons:

✜ to provide money for a home

✜ to give security for old age

✜ to provide for children

✜ to make leisure activities possible

✜ to give a sense of purpose, the feeling of a job well done

✜ for self-esteem

✤ to use your gifts and talents creatively

✤ to play a part in the life of the community

✤ to give status

✤ to meet people and make friends

✤ to have the means to give to others

✤ to serve God

There are so many reasons why we work. In our very pressurised society work can dominate a marriage. It can become the most important factor in life so that there is little time for fun, family and friends, and our only aim is to make our millions and retire early.

For the Christian, work can be part of our commitment and service to God. Some may feel called to a particular work, or to full-time Christian work, but in fact all work is Christian work for the person who belongs to Christ. 'Whatever you do, work at it with all your heart, as though you were working for the Lord and not for men' (Colossians 3:23).

If you can see your work as part of God's plan

for your life, it will add a new sense of purpose. Work, however, can cause problems in a marriage. If you go off to work early each morning, come home late and tired after a long journey, switch on the TV and sit in silence, your partner can start to feel left out and second best. You need to discuss together the work you believe God is asking you to do and to find out what your partner thinks and feels about this. And if one of you is out of work, that can be equally difficult, bringing feelings of depression and uselessness.

Let's look at some common problems relating to work:

✤ it can dominate your thoughts

✤ your partner is not interested in your job

✤ you feel you are of less importance than your partner's job

✤ there is no time for fun and friends

✤ the one left at home with children can feel left out

✤ there is great pressure to 'get on' at work

✣ you feel bored by your job

✣ you only feel a sense of value at work—not at home

As you think of your life together after marriage, talk about the work you do and try to understand what work is like for your partner. Discuss how you see your careers developing. If children come along, how will you feel at having to give up work and take care of them?

You are made in the image of a creator God, and work is his gift to enable you to use the brains and talents he has given you.

Discussion points

1. How important is your job to you?
2. How can you ensure you have enough quality time together when work, home care, family, church, friends and leisure activities will need your time as well?
3. In what way do you use the gifts God has given you in your work?
4. Do you see your work as part of your total Christian service, or is it divorced from your Christian activities? Do you need to change your attitude to work?

5. Are there any specific areas where your work might intrude or cause problems in your marriage? How will you deal with that?
6. What positive elements does your work bring into your relationship?
7. If you are out of work, discuss your feelings about that and the effect it is having on your relationship.

9
Leisure

~~~~~~~~~

'Oh, you're always round at the pub!'

'That's the third time you've been to your mother's this week!'

'Out with the girls again? When am I going to see you?'

'If you play football on Saturday and Sunday, and practise twice a week, we might as well not be married for all I see of you!'

One of the hardest areas to balance in your marriage will be leisure time spent with the friends you knew when you were single, your extended family, and spending time with each other and making new married friends.

Once upon a time you could go off and do your own thing without asking anyone for permission. Now there are two of you with different interests and hobbies on the one hand, and a real desire to be together and do things together on the other. And there is so much to do. With shorter working hours, leisure pursuits have led to a leisure industry—one of the fastest growing areas of modern life. There is plenty to tempt the eye and the pocket.

There are several reasons for setting aside time for leisure activities:

✤ to recoup your strength

✤ to get away from the pressures of work

✤ to have fun together

✤ to do things together

✤ to spend time with family and friends

When we were looking at the area of commitment, we saw that your relationship came second in priority to your relationship with God. This is important, and particularly so in the first year of marriage. However well you feel you know each other at the time of marriage, living constantly together will show you aspects about each other that you did not know before. The only answer to helping the two of you get to know each other better and to understand how the other ticks, is to spend *time together*. This is more to do with quality of time than quantity. One of the aims of your leisure time should be to have fun together.

For Christian couples it could be extremely helpful to say to your local church that you will not be available for any regular church work commitment during your first year of marriage. In the Old Testament God says that soldiers should have a year off from battles after they have married (Deuteronomy 24:5). This is a good principle.

God invented leisure. He rested on the seventh day of creation, and he specifically ordered it in the fourth commandment: 'In six days I, the Lord, made the earth, the sky, the sea, and everything in them, but on the seventh day I rested. That is why I, the Lord, blessed the Sabbath and made it holy' (Exodus 20:11).

Jesus emphasised this again and again when he saw his disciples tired and strained. He sent them off to recuperate, for he saw their need for recreation (a form of re-creation) as much as his own need for time alone to be with his Father.

However, you will also both need some separate leisure pursuits where you are able to keep up with old friends and hobbies. How much, and how often, is something you will need to sit down and discuss together, so that the day doesn't come when one of you sits at home seething while the other is out having a great time.

Discussion points

1. How important is it to you to keep up with your present hobbies and friends?
2. Your families will need to see you. How much time do you plan to devote to them?
3. Discuss the amount of time you think you will need to spend together, with no intrusion from television, telephone, or visitors.
4. How do you plan to have fun together?
5. What hobbies and interests can you share, and what do you plan to follow separately?

10
Sex

S ome couples will approach marriage already having had sex with each other. Many Christian couples will want to wait until they are married to consummate their relationship, for the Christian is aware that God specifically asks his people to keep the act of sexual intercourse within the marriage relationship. This is because intercourse is the expression of a total self-giving to the loved one, and is really only possible in that deep sense within the committed marriage relationship.

For the Christian who has had a sexual relationship outside marriage, remember that a new start is always possible, for God is your loving Father who, through the death of Jesus, can cleanse you from all sin.

It does happen that a couple have been living together and enjoying a reasonable sexual relationship, but that on marrying they are surprised to find that relationship deteriorates. This is because the dynamics of the partnership have changed. Marriage is about life-long commitment and responsibility, and that can feel like an awesome task. But within the security of that committed relationship, the physical relationship will have a chance to blossom and grow.

Whatever your experience, sex within marriage is a very special gift. Within the safety and security of marriage it is the outward physical expression of your deep love and commitment to one another.

Sexuality is God's gift to you.

He made you a man to enjoy your masculinity.

He made you a woman to enjoy your femininity.

Sexuality speaks about who you are and what you are, and gives you a sense of identity.

Sexual intercourse is God's gift to you as a couple. He did not give it in order for couples simply to have children but, as it says in the marriage service, 'that with delight and tenderness they may know each other in love, and, through the joy of their bodily union, may strengthen the union of their hearts and lives'. It is for the two of you to delight in each other's love and openness.

Sex is a glorious gift, but it can turn sour very easily. We are surrounded with talk and images of sex on the television, in films and magazines, and it is easy to think that all you have to do is get into bed and away you go! No problem! Sexual intercourse is a physical activity which you need to learn how to do for the maximum enjoyment, and this takes time. Yet you have the whole of your lives ahead of you, and indeed many couples in their forties and fifties find that their sexual relationship is better than ever before.

There are pressures that can make sex difficult:

✛ a fear of failure and not pleasing your partner

✛ ignorance of the differences between male and female arousal patterns

✛ being too eager and not giving time for the woman to get aroused, resulting in painful intercourse

✛ not having enough time

✛ being unable to talk about what you like and don't like

✛ problems of premature ejaculation

✣ the fear of being too rough and hurting your partner

Some of the pressures can be removed by reading helpful books about the sexual relationship. A *Touch of Love* by John and Janet Houghton (published by Kingsway) is especially helpful, though there are many others to help you with the techniques of love-making. Two Relate books are *The Relate Guide to Better Relationships* (Ebury Press, 1991) and *The Relate Guide to Sex in Loving Relationships* (Ebury Press, 1992), both by Sara Litvinoff.

If you are worried about any physical problems, have a word with your GP. He will then advise you what to do.

Discuss any fears you have together and with your local Family Planning Clinic, or go to Relate marriage guidance (formerly Marriage Guidance Council) or someone who is trained to help with any sexual problems you may be experiencing.

Don't try and discuss sexual problems while you are making love or just after. Leave it until later, over a cup of tea, when you are both more relaxed and have the time to think and to share your thoughts and feelings.

Remind yourself that intercourse is God's

special gift to you to deepen your love for each other. Take time to explore and enjoy each other's bodies and revel in your openness with each other. Bath or shower together, undress each other.

You may have traumas about intercourse which relate to some childhood experience. Talk together about this, and go and find professional help to enable you to work through the pains of the past.

Premature ejaculation is a common occurrence for the newly married male. As you become more secure in your relationship and learn to help your wife to respond, it should right itself eventually, and you will be able to get your timing right. Again, if you are anxious seek expert help, for there are simple exercises you can both be taught to help control ejaculation.

Learn together the different needs of husband and wife. Men are more easily aroused by sight. Women need to feel emotionally secure and loved in order to be aroused, and that takes longer. A good day, in which a woman has felt loved, will help her both to initiate and to respond to love-making. A woman doesn't always reach orgasm.

Don't expect to get it right straight away. Make it a fun time and learn to laugh together—not at each other.

Don't be afraid to try new ways of enjoying each other. Discuss openly what you like and what pleases you. Don't expect your partner to be a mind reader.

Be aware that having a child, pressure of work, tiredness and illness will all affect your sexual relationship. You need to make allowances for each other.

Make sure you are both happy with the contraception you are using. If not, go to the Family Planning clinic and discuss with them what would be better for you both.

Be sensitive to each other's needs.

Have a sense of humour.

Read the Song of Solomon together.

Discussion points

1. How important to you is sexual intercourse in the context of the rest of your life together?
2. How easy is it for you to talk to each other specifically about your sex life?
3. Can you share what you especially enjoy and find satisfying in your physical contact?

4. How often do you wish to make love? Are you both agreed on that?
5. Discuss any particular problems that you have.

II
Children

'I'd like a large family.'

'We can't afford children for at least eight years.'

'With the state of the world population it is immoral to have more than two children.'

'We've decided not to have any children, as we want to concentrate on our careers.'

No longer is having children something entirely beyond your control. This gives you the time you need to feel secure in your own relationship before contemplating having a child. No doubt you will have discussed well before the marriage your desire to have—or not to have—a family. It is important that you know each other's mind on this before the marriage. One of you, being sure that the other would go along with your feeling but without checking it out, could be in for an unpleasant surprise.

Some couples decide not to have children for a variety of reasons that may be valid for them. As Christians, if this is your decision, then it is good to look at your reasons closely; for implicit within God's design for marriage is the assumption that children will be born to the relationship and brought up in a secure and loving home.

In discussing when to have children, you will need to look at many facets of your life together. Can you afford them yet? It may mean losing one salary for a while at least. Do you feel able enough to cope with the extra demands made upon you in having children? Are you ready to give up being a twosome and become a threesome?

Consider some of the changes that having children brings:

✣ you become responsible for a totally dependent person

✣ time is no longer your own—it is governed by the baby's needs

✣ you will feel tired from broken nights

✣ you will need babysitters if you are to have time on your own

✣ there will be a lot of extra expense

✣ you will probably have to lose one income

✛ you can never be sure that plans will come to pass—the baby may be teething or unwell

✛ the wife will need a lot of patience and support from her husband, and may not be too interested in sex for a while

✛ the husband may feel left out and missing regular sex as the baby's needs come first

✛ wherever you go there will be all the paraphernalia to take as well

But set against that are the joys of having children:

✛ the wonder of being part of God's plan of creation

✛ the joy that the fruit of your love has produced a child

✛ watching your child grow from baby to toddler to child to adolescent to adult

✛ being a family

✛ seeing your own characteristics in your child

Be aware that in the joy of having children there can be pain also, for it is seldom straightforward, and for as long as you live you will always be concerned for your child.

Discussion points

1. Discuss the good and bad things about your own childhood. How did your parents handle feelings, especially anger? Do you want to be the same sort of parents, or are there some things you want to do differently?
2. What are your feelings about disciplining children?
3. How do you feel you would cope if your child had some problem, handicap or emotional difficulty?
4. If you find you cannot have children, and yet you want them, what will you do? Will you seek medical advice, or consider adoption?

T hus far you have looked at various areas in your relationship together, and have discussed your attitudes to them. The last two chapters— Communication and Faith—look at the most important aspects of your life together.

You will be able to manage the different areas of your life only if you are able to communicate adequately with each other. And as Christians, the fact of your faith in God and how you work that out in your everyday life will decide whether you live a life just for yourselves, or whether your life has Jesus right in the centre of your home, guiding you and surrounding you with his love.

12

Communication

W e use words to express what is going on in our minds. What we say—the words we use—conveys our thoughts and feelings.

But the way in which we say things can also communicate. The intonation we use may change the meaning of the words, and our facial expressions will tell their own story: a frown, a grin, and so on. We also communicate with our body language, and your partner will ascertain a great deal from a tenseness in your body or a droop of your shoulders. Silence too can be a powerful means of communication.

As you learn to know each other better, so you will pick up from each other many non-verbal messages that will let you know how loved and accepted you are, whether you are being listened to, whether your partner is coping with your anger or your excitement.

It takes time to understand the messages correctly, and at first you may feel frustrated with each other as you are not sure what your partner is trying to say to you. Or you simply may not hear. You may accuse each other of being insensitive and not caring, because messages of need are not coming through clearly enough.

Communication in every area is vital. That is why it is so important that at the start of your life together you give yourselves enough time to talk, listen, and understand what is in each other's hearts. And this will be needed right through your marriage relationship for however long it lasts.

As years go by people change and grow, and in order to keep your marriage intact and alive, you need to spend time—just the two of you—listening and understanding. Life can become more and more busy, but time spent on marriage maintenance is never wasted and will enrich your relationship. And if you have children, a relationship that is alive and well will give them the right environment for growth.

For really good communication you need:

✛ enough time. An evening once a week, for example, or whatever is right for you both.

✛ no distractions. No television, telephone calls or visitors—just the two of you.

✤ to be prepared to listen. If there is a grievance voiced you need to hear what the problem is and discuss it. You both need to feel that you have been listened to.

✤ to be prepared to talk. One of you may find it easier than the other to use words to describe your feelings. Be patient. Even if it does not come naturally, try to find the words to convey how you feel.

✤ to accept each other as you are. You can't change one another.

✤ to accept that there may be times of anger. One or both of you may be wary of confrontation and anger, but there is always the chance to say sorry and to forgive.

✤ to accept that each of you is different. You are from different backgrounds and have different needs and fears. You won't always be able to meet all of each other's needs.

✤ to be lovingly open with each other.

Like learning how to please each other sexually, so also you will find yourselves learning how to communicate adequately. It is a good feeling when not only your bodies learn the language of love, but your hearts and minds learn the language of clear and loving communication.

Things do go wrong. There will be times in your marriage when you feel a black cloud between you; when you are angry with each other; when communicating seems to be the last thing you can do. That doesn't mean your marriage is over. It means that you need to take time out together to look at what is going on. Sometimes you may need a third person to help you sort things out. It is not advisable to involve family or friends—but an impartial marriage counsellor can help you to get things into perspective. As Christians coming to the cross of Jesus Christ, you will find there—

✛ acceptance and love for who you are as individuals and as a couple.

✛ forgiveness for each of you, and the power to forgive each other.

✛ cleansing and peace for your relationship.

✛ the strength, courage and power of the Holy Spirit to start again.

At such times it may be helpful to read prayerfully together a psalm such as Psalm 51:

> Be merciful to me, O God,
> because of your constant love.
> Because of your great mercy wipe away my sins!
> . . . I recognise my faults;
> I am always conscious of my sins.
> . . . Sincerity and truth are what you require;
> fill my mind with your wisdom.
> . . . Let me hear the sounds of joy and gladness;
> and though you have crushed me and broken me,
> I will be happy once again.

Discussion points

1. How open were your family in discussing feelings and emotions? Were you allowed to get angry? If so, how was anger resolved?
2. How well can you handle someone else's anger?
3. Do you find it easy to forgive and forget when someone has hurt you?
4. Are you prepared to be the one who says 'I'm sorry' first?

13
Faith

―――――∞∞∞∞∞――――――

'A s for me and my family, we will serve the Lord' (Joshua 24:15). Joshua's statement is one of clear intent on his part that the sovereign Lord would be the head of his family and would be the One they would look to for guidance in every part of their lives.

Right at the start of your marriage, in the wedding service, it says, 'We have come together in the presence of God. . . .' That is a clear statement by the two of you that you are not only coming before God for his blessing on your life together, but that together you want to set up a Christian home where Jesus Christ is at the centre of your life and the head of your home.

You need to talk together about your experience of Christianity. Is Jesus real in your life? What helps you keep close to God? You need to share your experiences of church life and activity. You may have met at church and so had similar experiences, or you may come from different churches that express faith in Jesus in different forms of worship. You may be feeling that your faith is weak and that you have little under-standing. Share these feelings.

Now you are to be married it will still be you as an individual in your relationship with Jesus. That will still need to be guarded and nurtured so that you continue to grow as a Christian and increase in faith and understanding. But it will also be you, the couple, the family, in relation-ship with Jesus. You need to work out how your faith can draw you closer to each other and to the Lord, and how you can be a witness to those you will live among in the neighbourhood.

There are various ways in which you can encourage your faith to grow:

✢ Find a church. You may have moved away from your home church. It is important to find a church that both of you can worship in and find fellowship in as soon as possible.

✢ Introduce yourself to the pastor or vicar, explaining that you want to worship there, although you do not want any positions of responsibility in the church during your first year of marriage. Some clergy are very eager to put people to work at once.

✣ Join a home-group fellowship where you can find support and companionship.

✣ Keep up your own prayer life and your own individual study of God's word.

✣ Make time each day to pray together and bring to the Lord all the things in your heart.

✣ Consider saying grace at mealtimes to remind yourselves that God is the provider of all good things.

✣ Seek the Lord's guidance together on how you spend your time, your money, and how you work out your roles.

✣ Talk to God about your work, and about when to have children.

✣ Thank God together for his gift to you of sexual intimacy.

✣ Find other couples with whom you can share your faith and failures.

✣ Say 'sorry' when you hurt each other.

It has been said that a couple who pray together, stay together. More true is the fact that at the cross of Jesus you can—individually and as a couple—bring the hurts you have inflicted on each other, the pains and the wounds of the past, your inadequacies, fears and needs, and find his forgiveness, cleansing and healing. And he will pour into your hearts his Holy Spirit to assure you that you are his beloved sons and daughters.

Read together Psalm 16—noting particularly verse 11:

> You will show me the path that leads to life;
> your presence fills me with joy
> and brings me pleasure for ever.

Discussion points

1. Do you find it easy to pray out loud together? How can you help each other to do this more naturally?
2. How can you help each other to love Jesus, to serve him, to worship him?
3. Are there areas of faith on which you disagree? Do you think either of you needs to change, or can you live with those differences?
4. How do you think you can use your home in God's service?

14

Conclusion

You have thought through different areas of your life together. Spend some time now offering up yourselves and your relationship to the Lord. Your special day is approaching. Read through together the words you will be saying to one another:

> To have and to hold
> from this day forward;
> for better, for worse,
> for richer, for poorer,
> in sickness and in health,
> to love and to cherish,
> till death us do part,
> according to God's holy law;
> and this is my solemn vow.

As you think about these words, read again together 1 Corinthians 13:

Love is patient and kind; it is not jealous or conceited or proud; love is not ill-mannered or selfish or irritable; love does not keep a record of wrongs; love is not happy with evil, but is happy with the truth. Love never gives up; and its faith, hope and patience never fail.

Love is eternal.

May God the Father,
God the Son,
God the Holy Spirit
bless, preserve and keep you
the Lord mercifully grant you the riches of his grace that you may please him in both body and soul, and living together in faith and love, may receive the blessings of eternal life. Amen.